Design Your Morning Routine

Jump-Start Your Writing Success

Author Success Foundations Book 2

by

Christopher di Armani

Editor: Nicolas Johnson

Published By:
Botanie Valley Productions Inc.
PO Box 507
Lytton, BC V0K 1Z0
http://BotanieValleyProductions.com

Dedication

This book is dedicated to my sweet and loving wife Lynda.

Without her unwavering support none of this would be possible.

Acknowledgments

Without the assistance of my editor, Nicolas Johnson, I can't imagine how this book would read. He tears my words apart from every conceivable angle, then offers thoughtful and constructive criticism on how best to fix the destruction at our feet. I thank God for Nicolas Johnson and his talents, daily.

#EditorsMatter

Feedback Loop

I also wish to express my heartfelt gratitude to the following individuals who took time from their own busy lives to critique this manuscript. Their willingness to assist a total stranger humbles me.

Kim Steadman (KimSteadman.com)
Sharilee Swaity (Facebook.com/Sharilee.Swaity)

Table of Contents

Foreword

Imagine you wake up tomorrow with a clear focus for your life.

Imagine you wake up tomorrow certain this is your most productive day ever.

Imagine you wake up tomorrow confident the action you take today will move you one step closer to your ultimate goal - your published book.

Now think about how you woke up this morning.

Did the alarm clock shock you awake? Did you slam the snooze button in frustration, desperate for a few more minutes of sleep? Did you drag your butt out of bed, stagger into the kitchen and discover the coffee can is empty? Did you drag your butt out the door, late for work, as always?

Did you try to figure out what you need to accomplish today, but fail? Did you wonder if you could find time to write at all? Did the grumbling voice in the back of your mind whisper, once again, your dream of a publish book is just a childish fantasy?

If these questions resonate with you, you're in the right place.

You can wake up every day focused on your goal.

You can wake up every day, certain you can write more words than you wrote yesterday, and write them easier and faster, too.

You can wake up every day with greater clarity of purpose.

You can wake up every day eager to move one step closer to your published book.

A bold promise? No, a simple statement of fact.

It all starts with your morning routine.

Yes, you already have a morning routine. It may be unplanned and chaotic, but it is still a routine. A few simple changes will improve your focus, clarity and productivity for the rest of your day, and for the rest of your life.

There is no magic to writing a book. None. You take action, every single day, until your book is finished. You plan, schedule and execute the plan. You write.

Simple.

This book teaches you how to begin your day with clarity.

You will learn specific habits to improve your focus and remove needless decisions from your day entirely.

You must participate in every exercise to achieve the greatest results.

If you are serious about finishing your manuscript, grab your notebook, a pen, and a cup of your favorite beverage, and join me at the kitchen table. We'll chat about habits, willpower and self-discipline. We'll discuss how the mind functions, what makes a habit stick, and how our willpower fades throughout the day. We'll talk about concrete steps to improve your self-discipline.

Then I'll ask you to complete a series of exercises. These exercises reveal, at a deep level, what's important to you - what you value most in life. This clarity of purpose allows you to create a morning routine designed to jump-start your daily writing output.

Don't worry. I don't tell you what to do.

I offer suggestions.

I encourage you to begin with small changes to experience immediate "wins." I will show you how other productive writers start their days and ask you to add key elements from their lives to your daily routine.

Pick what works for you and forget about the rest.

But this whole process begins with honesty - self-honesty - so grab a full bucket of willingness and let's get started.

Chapter 1

The Power of Habit

Habit Defined

Having a set routine where I do the same things at the same time every day is crucial to saving time and mental energy.

– Jessica Dang

Webster's 9th New Collegiate Dictionary defines habit as:

1. A behavior pattern acquired by frequent repetition or physiological exposure that shows itself in regularity or increased facility of performance

2. A way of acting fixed through repetition

3. An acquired move of behavior that has become nearly involuntary.

When we perform a series of tasks without conscious thought, we perform by habit. We are not zombies, though. We are aware of our actions, but the impulse to perform them is unconscious and, when deeply ingrained, compulsive. Watch a child as they learn how to walk. Their focus is incredible. When I was a baby I focused on how to put one foot in front of the other without falling flat on my face, to the exclusion of everything else.

As an adult, I do not focus on the physiological commands necessary for my body to stand, walk to the kitchen and pour a fresh cup of coffee. I perform these actions automatically. Once I learned these skills as a child, my mind shifted them into my subconscious mind. It performs them flawlessly, when required.

Do you remember when you learned how to drive? Your single-minded focus filled your mind with a non-stop barrage of questions. How do I press the gas and release the clutch at the same time so I don't stall the engine? Is it safe to change lanes? Why did the windshield wipers turn on? How do I stop them?

These skills took immense concentration to master. With practice and experience, they became second nature. They became habit.

Think about your daily commute. Unless an unusual event occurs to jar you out of this routine and unconscious act, you don't remember the drive to or from work each day.

This is the power of habit. Out goal is to perform our morning routine with this same efficiency, with the same lack of conscious thought, so our conscious mind can focus its energy upon what matters - writing.

The 21-Day Myth

Feeling sorry for yourself and your present condition is not only a waste of energy but the worst habit you could possibly have.

— Dale Carnegie

In his blockbuster hit Psycho-Cybernetics, author and cosmetic surgeon Dr. Maxwell Maltz wrote the following:

> "It usually requires a minimum of about 21 days to effect any perceptible change in a mental image. Following plastic surgery it takes about 21 days for the average patient to get used to his new face. When an arm or leg is amputated, the 'phantom limb' persists for about 21 days. People must live in a new house for about three weeks before it begins to 'seem like home.' These and many other commonly observed phenomena tend to show that it requires a minimum of about 21 days for an old mental image to dissolve and a new one to jell." [1]

Self-help gurus latched on to Maltz's 21 days concept, but deleted his all-important phrase "a minimum of" when they rewrote his words into this mantra:

"It requires 21 days to form a new habit."

Contrary to this persistent myth, 21 days is the minimum time required to form a new habit, not the maximum, nor even the average.

Researchers studied habit formation after his misinterpreted quote went viral. Their peer-reviewed research confirmed "21 days to a new habit" is a well-intentioned fantasy, nothing more, and true habit formation takes much longer.

In his study *Making Health Habitual: The Psychology of Habit Formation and General Practice,* Benjamin Gardner concluded[2] it required an average of 66 days to form a new habit.

"Participants in one study repeated a self-chosen health-promoting behaviour (for example, eat fruit, go for a walk) in response to a single, once-daily cue in their own environment (such as, after breakfast). Daily ratings of the subjective automaticity of the behaviour (that is, habit strength) showed an asymptotic increase, with an initial acceleration that slowed to a plateau after an average of 66 days."

Another study, *How Are Habits Formed: Modelling Habit Formation in the Real World,* conducted by Phillipa Lally,[3] determined it can take as little as 18 days and as much as 254 days to build a new habit.

The time required varies from person to person. When you want to build a new habit, Gardner's average of 66 days is a useful model. It ensures you practice your new behavior every day and hold off your evaluation for two months before you assess if your new behavior is now an unconscious and effective action, or habit.

Habit Benefits

Repetition is the reality and the seriousness of life.

— Soren Kierkegaard

Benjamin Gardner, the researcher who discovered it takes, on average, 66 days to build a new habit, explained the benefits of habits in his 2012 article *Busting The 21 Days Habit Formation Myth.*[4]

We know habits are formed through a process called 'context-dependent repetition'. For example, imagine that, each time you get home each evening, you eat a snack. When you first eat the snack upon getting home, a mental link is formed between the context (getting home) and your response to that context (eating a snack). Each time you subsequently snack in response to getting home, this link strengthens, to the point that getting home comes to prompt you to eat a snack automatically, without giving it much prior thought; a habit has formed.

Habits are mentally efficient: the automation of frequent behaviours allows us to conserve the mental resources that we would otherwise use to monitor and control these behaviours, and deploy them on more difficult or novel tasks. Habits are likely to persist over time; because they are automatic and so do not rely on conscious thought, memory or willpower.

Your morning routine automates positive behaviors at the start of your day. These habits reduce your stress level before the real work begins and this positive effect carries over into every activity for the rest of your day.

It's a powerful motivator to design and build a morning routine, then stick to it. Another quote from Benjamin Gardner explains this in the context of New Year's resolutions.

The bottom line is: stay strong. 21 days is a myth; habit formation typically takes longer than that. The best estimate is 66 days, but it's unwise to attempt to assign a number to this process. The duration of habit formation is likely to differ depending on who you are and what you are trying to do. As long as you continue doing your new healthy behaviour consistently in a given situation, a habit will form. But you will probably have to persevere beyond January 21st.

Habits are powerful because they bolster our willpower and, contrary to another myth, willpower is a muscle. The more you exercise it, the stronger it becomes.

Willpower is a Muscle

Willpower is what separates us from the animals. It's the capacity to restrain our impulses, resist temptation – do what's right and good for us in the long run, not what we want to do right now. It's central, in fact, to civilization.

— Dr. Roy Baumeister, Ph. D.

Willpower is a finite resource.

Our willpower is weakest in the hours prior to mealtimes, lunch and dinner. This is also when our glucose levels are lowest. Conversely, our willpower is strongest after a good night's sleep and a healthy breakfast.

Digestion produces glucose which is converted into neurotransmitters (the chemical messengers powering our mind and body) and pushed into our blood stream. When we don't eat regularly, we run low on glucose and the neurotransmitters created from it.

When we run low on neurotransmitters, we no longer think clearly. We no longer make good decisions.

Dr. Baumeister conducted a series of laboratory experiments where he "rediscovered" the force we call willpower. He learned how willpower gives people the strength to persevere, how they lose self-control as their willpower is depleted, and how willpower is fueled by the glucose in the body's bloodstream. He and his collaborators also discovered that willpower, like a muscle, becomes fatigued from overuse but can also be strengthened through regular exercise.[5]

In his bestselling book *Willpower: Why Self-Control is the Secret to Success*[6], Dr. Baumeister discussed a fascinating Israeli study[7] which discovered judges granted parole more often to a person early in the day, when their glucose levels remained high. They did not grant parole to almost identical cases late in the afternoon, when their glucose levels fell.

He cites four cases from the study - two men convicted of fraud and two men convicted of assault - and explains how the first man convicted of fraud was granted parole but not the second. The same happened with the two men convicted of assault - the first was granted parole but not the second.

❑ Case 1 (heard at 8:50 A.M.): An Arab-Israeli male serving a 30-month sentence for fraud.

❑ Case 2 (heard at 1:27 P.M.): A Jewish-Israeli male serving a 16-month sentence for assault.

❑ Case 3 (heard at 3:10 P.M.): A Jewish-Israeli male serving a 16-month sentence for assault.

❑ Case 4 (heard at 4:25 P.M.): An Arab-Israeli male serving a 30-month sentence for fraud.

In both sets of cases, judges granted the prisoner parole soon after a meal break. In both instances where parole was denied, judges heard the cases late in the afternoon session, when glucose levels reached their lowest point and decision fatigue reached its highest.

> "To be sure, mealtimes were not the only thing that predicted the outcome of the rulings. Offenders who appeared prone to recidivism (in this case those with previous convictions) were more likely to be turned down, as were those who were not in a rehabilitation programme. Happily, neither the sex nor the ethnicity of the prisoners seemed to matter to the judges. Nor did the length of time the offenders already spent in prison, nor even the severity of their crimes (as assessed by a separate panel of legal experts). But after controlling for recidivism and rehabilitation programmes, the meal-related pattern remained."

The Israeli study also noted the following:

> Two further findings buttress the idea that it is the psychological load of decision making which matters.

> First, the average unfavourable decision (unfavourable to the prisoner, that is) took less time to arrive at (5.2 minutes) than the average favourable one (7.4 minutes). Second, it also took more time to explain. Written verdicts in favourable rulings averaged 90 words, compared with just 47 for unfavourable ones.

Decision Fatigue

Whenever you see a successful business, someone once made a courageous decision.

— Peter F. Drucker

In *Willpower*[9], Dr. Baumeister explains how decision fatigue causes us to make poor decisions, despite our best intentions.

> The problem of decision fatigue affects everything from the careers of CEOs to the prison sentences of felons appearing before weary judges. It influences the behavior of everyone, executive and non-executive, every day. Yet few people are even aware of it. When asked whether making decisions would deplete their willpower

and make them vulnerable to temptation, most people say no. They don't realize that decision fatigue helps explain why ordinarily sensible people get angry at their colleagues and families, splurge on clothes, buy junk food at the supermarket, and can't resist the car dealer's offer to rustproof their new sedan.

The primary benefit of a morning routine is our lowered susceptibility to decision fatigue for the rest of our day. When we remove decisions from our mornings, we reserve more power to make correct decisions later.

This is why it is critical to tackle our most difficult task first. Our willpower and ability to make sound decisions are at their peak at the start of our day. Better decisions lead to higher quality work.

The Power of Self-Discipline

The key to accepting responsibility for your life is to accept the fact that your choices, every one of them, are leading you inexorably to either success or failure, however you define those terms.

— Neal Boortz

Success is determined, not by your intelligence (or lack thereof), but by your self-discipline.

A study conducted by Angela L. Duckworth and Martin E. P. Seligman[10] showed students who exerted high levels of willpower were more likely to earn higher grades and gain admission into better post-education schools.

> Highly self-disciplined adolescents outperformed their more impulsive peers on every academic-performance variable. Self-discipline predicted academic performance more robustly than did IQ. Self-discipline also predicted which students would improve their grades over the course of the school year, whereas IQ did not.... Self-discipline has a bigger effect on academic performance than does intellectual talent.

When we apply self-discipline and make sound decisions, we build the muscles of our willpower. This allows us to make better decisions over longer periods of time. It is simple to create a solid morning routine, but it is not easy. It is simple to determine what to do. It is not easy because we must apply self-discipline to implement our routine.

We must force ourselves to build our new activities into solid habits. It requires self-discipline. The benefits of this foundation are immense. We remain calm and focused for longer. We write more words per day in less time. Our daily word count increases, and so does the quality of our work.

I want to write more quality words in less time. How about you?

Reactive vs Proactive Mornings

It's been said that the first hour is the rudder of the day. I've found this to be very true in my own life. If I'm lazy or haphazard in my actions during the first hour after I wake up, I tend to have a fairly lazy and unfocused day.

– Steve Pavlina

A reactive morning is one without focus, without a designed intent or outcome. Before I learned the difference and taught myself how to build a proper, proactive morning routine, here's what my day looked like.

I woke up. Not to an alarm, but whenever I opened my eyes. I checked my email and waded through the daily influx of spam, irrelevant email sales pitches, news and bright shiny objects. I followed every flight of fancy on my Facebook and Twitter feeds. Most days I made a cup of coffee and drank it as I frittered even more time away on social media.

Some mornings I would read the Bible, some days I wouldn't. I sure didn't pray with regularity or express my gratitude for the many blessings in my life, not even my ability to write.

Eventually, I would stop procrastinating and start writing. Eventually.

The entire process could take as long as five hours, but seldom took less than two. And this was my daily routine after I quit my day job to write full time. Pathetic. Writing was my job, but I lacked the focus and discipline required to get things done.

A proactive morning is a different animal. Every step of my morning routine now serves a designed purpose. I plan it all in advance, so when my alarm goes off, I get out of bed and complete a specific series of tasks on autopilot, no thinking required.

Through my daily application of self-discipline these became healthy habits, the key to a purpose-driven morning routine.

What is a Morning Routine and Why do I Need One?

Excellence…is not an act, but a habit.

— Aristotle's Nicomachean Ethics (Book II, 4; Book I, 7).

A well-designed morning routine frees you up to be your most productive self. It defines and clarifies your priorities and purpose. A routine puts your body on autopilot and frees your mind to focus on the most important tasks of your day – whatever they are – and drive your book another mile down Publication Highway.

Willpower ebbs and flows throughout the day, as does your ability to make correct decisions.

Many writers abhor structure. They believe it sucks creativity from their lives.

Good structure does the opposite. It frees your mind to unlock its full creative potential.

Structure, like plot in the stories you write, is the skeleton of your day. It is the mast upon which you hang your sail. Take away this structure and you are a sailboat without a mast. You lack the ability to chart your own course. Instead, you drift whichever way the current flows.

Isn't the ability to chart our own course in life the essence of creativity?

Chapter 2

Take The Morning Routine Test

Start With Self-Honesty

Life is about choices. Some we regret, some we're proud of. Some will haunt us forever. The message? We are what we choose to be.

— Graham Brown

If we keep doing what we always did, we will keep getting the same unsatisfying results.

Great grammar and sentence composition? Hardly.

But it makes an undeniable point.

You didn't buy this book because your writing life is focused, productive and fulfilling. You bought it because your life is the opposite - unfocused, unproductive and unfulfilling. Your pain and dissatisfaction forced you to find a solution to these problems.

You know, deep in your heart, you can write more, write better, and write faster, even though you don't right now. You bought this book because you're tired of your publishing dreams being, well, an unfulfilled fantasy. You want to turn your dreams into reality.

In light of this, two things become critical.

First, you must evaluate where you are now, with honesty and diligence.

Second, you must change how you work.

Don't kid yourself. You already have a morning routine. Everyone does. Most people don't do these things by design and, with the help of this book, you can make conscious choices about the activities you perform each day.

Before you can design a new, more effective routine, you must understand your current one. Only then can you make the choice to improve it.

This is the purpose of the Morning Routine Test.

Grab your notebook and a pen, and answer the questions ahead. Beside each answer, add the point value for it. When you are done, add up your score. Don't worry - nobody will ever see your answers. This is a tool to evaluate your current morning routine so you can build a more effective one. That's all.

To become more productive writers we must make decisions about our lives based on fact. We must move ourselves away from our current non-productive state and shift to a more creative and fruitful one.

Every step of the way is simple. As with most things of value in this life, simple does not always equate to easy. Change is hard due to our internal resistance to it. Thankfully, we can overcome both our internal resistance to change and the external forces aligned against us, as well.

How?

We'll get to those answers shortly, but first, take The Morning Routine Test.

The Morning Routine Test

The Morning Routine Test is a series of questions designed to show you if your current morning routine builds a solid foundation for a productive day. In your notebook, write down your answers to each of the following questions, and how long it takes you to accomplish each task.

If you prefer to use a pre-written test, download the worksheet from here:

https://ChristopherDiArmani.net/morning-routine-test

Ready?

Great. Let's get started.

The Morning Routine Test

1. I write or edit every day except Sundays. A day of rest is a great thing and helps recharge my batteries.

How often do you write? Do you write every day?

- ❑ Yes, I write every day of the week = 10 Points
- ❑ No, I write 6 days per week. I take one day off = 10 Points
- ❑ No, I take two days off each week = 8 Points
- ❑ No, I only write 3 or 4 days per week = 5 Points
- ❑ No, I only write 1 or 2 days per week = 2 Points

2. How much time do you set aside for writing each day?

The purpose of this test is to face facts. There is no other way to make rational decisions about how to best move forward. Nobody wants to admit how little time they set aside for writing. If you have a spouse, a full-time job and one or more children, it's hard to set aside time to write. I get it, but this is the time for brutal honesty.

How much time do you set aside to write each day?

- ❑ 120 minutes or more = 10 Points
- ❑ 90 minutes = 8 Points
- ❑ 60 minutes = 6 Points
- ❑ 30 minutes = 4 Points
- ❑ I don't write every day = 2 Points

The next set of questions deal with your current daily morning routine.

3. Before you go to sleep at night, do you select your wardrobe for the next day?

- ❑ Yes, every night = 10 Points
- ❑ Yes, most nights = 8 Points
- ❑ No, not consistently = 4 Points
- ❑ No = 0 Points

4. Before you go to sleep at night, do you make a list of the three most important tasks you must complete the next day?

- ❑ Yes, every night = 10 Points
- ❑ Yes, most nights = 8 Points
- ❑ No, not consistently = 4 Points
- ❑ No = 0 Points

5. I am not a morning person, but even I can't ignore the conclusions of multiple studies showing that morning people are more productive, on average, than night owls like me.

I attempt to earn points for this question, but fail more often than I succeed.

If you score zero on this question, don't feel bad. I do too.

What time do you wake up?

- ❑ 6am or earlier = 10 Points
- ❑ 7am - 7am = 9 Points
- ❑ 7am - 8am = 8 Points
- ❑ 8am - 9am = 6 Points
- ❑ Whenever I want = 0 Points

6. How many hours do you sleep per night, on average?

- ❑ 8 hours or more = 10 points
- ❑ 7 hours - 8 hours = 7 points
- ❑ 6 hours - 7 hours = 3 points
- ❑ Less than 6 hours = 0 points

7. Where is your phone when you go to bed at night?

In another room of the house = 10 Points

- ❑ Turned off = 10 Points
- ❑ Beside my bed as my alarm clock on Airplane Mode = 10 Points
- ❑ In my bedroom, across the room and out of reach = 4 Points
- ❑ Beside my bed = 0 Points

8. How do you wake up each day?

- ❑ Naturally, when the sun wakes me up = 10 points
- ❑ With an alarm clock using a gentle sound = 8 points
- ❑ With an alarm clock using an annoying beep = 3 points
- ❑ With the radio tuned to the morning news = 2 point
- ❑ Whenever I wake up is when I wake up = 0 points

9. Do you hit the snooze button? More than once?

- ❑ No, I get out of bed as soon as my alarm goes off = 10 Points
- ❑ No, but I don't get out of bed right away either = 5 Points
- ❑ Yes, most days = 2 Points
- ❑ Yes, at least twice, sometimes more = 0 Points

10. What about The Elixir Of Life? Do you drink coffee or tea in the morning? One cup? Two? More than two?

- ❑ No, I don't need coffee or tea to wake up = 10 Points
- ❑ Yes, I drink one cup (black) in the morning = 8 Points
- ❑ Yes, I drink one cup with cream and/or sugar in the morning = 7 Points
- ❑ Yes, I drink two cups in the morning = 6 Points
- ❑ Yes, three or more cups = 0 Points

11. Do you watch the morning television news?

- ❑ No = 10 Points
- ❑ Yes, I need to know what's happening in the world = 0 Points

12. Do you read the newspaper (physical or digital) or other online news site in the morning?

- ❑ No = 10 Points
- ❑ Yes, I need to know what's happening in the world = 0 Points

13. Do you listen to the radio in the morning?

- ❑ No = 10 Points
- ❑ Yes, I listen to the radio = 0 Points

14. What about email, Facebook and Twitter? Do you log on to social media in the morning?

- ❏   No = 10 points
- ❏   Yes, I log on to social media for 30 minutes or less = 3 points
- ❏   Yes, I log on to social media for more than 30 minutes = 2 points
- ❏   Yes, I'm on social media from the time I wake up = 0 points

15. Do you shower in the morning or at night before you go to bed?

- ❏   Yes = 10 Points
- ❏   No = 5 Points

16. If you shower, how long does it take you?

- ❏   10 minutes or less = 10 points
- ❏   15 minutes = 5 points
- ❏   Longer than 15 minutes. Waking up is hard = 2 points

17. Do you brush and floss your teeth in the morning?

- ❏   Yes = 10 Points
- ❏   Yes, both most days = 10 Points
- ❏   Sometimes, but not consistently = 5 Points
- ❏   No = 0 Points

18. If you brush and floss your teeth, how long does it normally take you?

- ❏   Minimum of 2 minutes but less than 5 minutes = 10 points
- ❏   Longer than 5 minutes = 7 points

19. Do you eat breakfast, or is coffee your breakfast?

- ❏   Yes, I eat breakfast = 10 points
- ❏   No, I can't face food before 10am = 0 points

20. What do you eat for breakfast?

- ❑   A protein shake or smoothie = 10 Points
- ❑   A selection of fresh fruit = 10 Points
- ❑   Oatmeal = 10 Points
- ❑   Yogurt (with or without fruit) = 10 Points
- ❑   Bacon/sausages & eggs = 10 Points
- ❑   Toast (with anything on it) = 5 Points
- ❑   Anything else = 2 Points

21. Do you exercise in the morning (6 days per week)?

- ❑   Yes, for at least 30 minutes = 20 Points
- ❑   Yes, for at least 15 minutes = 15 Points
- ❑   Yes, for about 10 minutes = 10 Points
- ❑   Yes, but not every morning = 5 point
- ❑   I'm lucky if I wake up in time to leave for work! = 0 Points

22. Do you drink a 16oz glass of water in the morning after you wake up?

- ❑   Yes, every day = 20 Points
- ❑   Yes, but not every day = 10 Points
- ❑   Coffee has water. Does that count? = 0 Points

23. For most people, a mug of coffee and the morning paper is the closest they come to quiet time or meditation. Do you spend any quiet time in meditation and/or daily devotions in the morning?

- ❑   Yes, every morning for 15 minutes = 20 Points
- ❑   Yes, every morning for 10 minutes or less = 10 Points
- ❑   Yes, but not on a regular basis = 5 Points
- ❑   What are meditation and daily devotions? = 0 Points

24. Do you create and go over your gratitude list in the morning?

☐   Yes, every day = 20 Points

☐   No, but I spend some time thinking about what I'm grateful for each morning = 15 Points

☐   Sometimes, but not every day = 10 Points

☐   No = 0 Points

25. Do you make a list of priorities for the day ahead or review the list you made the night before?

☐   Yes, every morning = 10 points

☐   Yes, sometimes = 5 points

☐   No, it's a total waste of time = 0 points

26. Do you do anything to prepare for the following day before you go to bed at night?

☐   Yes, every night = 10 Points

☐   Yes, but not every night = 6 Points

☐   No. Who has time? = 0 Points

Is Your Morning Designed for Success?

With all the answers in front of you, it's time to add up the points and see where you stand.

If your score is between 0 and 105, your morning routine is on life support in the Intensive Care Unit.

If your score is between 106 and 155, your morning routine has a few positive aspects, but is in need of serious assistance.

If your score is between 156 and 205, you're doing a few things right, but there is a lot of room for improvement.

If your score is 206 or higher, you're doing great. See if there is any part of your morning routine you can tweak to raise your score even higher.

While this test is not scientific, it is based upon published research into what makes an individual more productive throughout their day.

Conclusion

Before you can change your current system and schedule more time to write, you need to understand what constitutes a productivity-oriented morning routine.

With your test score in mind, read through the following chapter to learn about 28 morning habits you can implement to increase your productivity.

Don't try to implement every suggestion. It's impossible. Focus on habits to keep your body healthy and your mind calm.

How I start my day holds immense power over the rest of my day.

Before I understood that simple truth, my morning routine sucked. If this test existed then, my score would not break 100 points. Today, I score a respectable 292, but I still have a lot of room for improvement.

It's a journey, not a destination.

And on my best days, I'm still a backsliding disaster.

Chapter 3

28 Morning Habits of Highly Successful People

28 Suggestions, Not 28 Commandments

Success leaves clues and the road to excellence is simple. Learn what successful people do and emulate their actions in your own life.

Every item on this list came from the morning routines of successful writers and business people. If these activities work for them, perhaps they can work for you too.

These are suggestions, not Commandments. You don't need to incorporate them all. You don't even need to include most of them. Pick the ideas you resonate with and build from there.

Take your current morning routine, whatever it may be, and eliminate those items you know are not beneficial. Replace them with something from this list.

I described my own time-wasting morning routine back in Chapter 1, remember? It didn't change overnight. Bad habits developed over years don't vanish in a day, but with self-discipline and dedication, good habits replaced the bad. Over time I became happier and more productive.

If you are not religious, you may choose to ignore the prayer and Bible options and, instead, focus on your attitude of gratitude, motivational books and meditation options.

If you are religious, daily prayer, Bible reading and meditation are great additions to your routine. If, for example, you read three chapters of the Bible each day, which takes about 15 minutes, you will read the entire Bible once each year.

The following suggestions are not listed in any particular order.

Remember to Cut Yourself Some Slack

Change is difficult.

Don't be discouraged if you balk at it. Resistance to change is natural and normal. If you don't meet your expectations one morning, be gentle with yourself. Resolve to do better tomorrow, and follow through on your commitment.

Allow self-discipline to be your friend.

Do what you know you should do, when you know you should do it, even when you don't feel like it.

In short order, your sense of pride in accomplishment will build your self-discipline. As with all habits, the more you practice your productive morning routine the easier it becomes.

Plan Your Wardrobe the Night Before

Spend 15 minutes to select tomorrow's wardrobe before you go to bed at night and you will remove one of the biggest headaches from your morning.

Why is this important?

Stress reduction. When you are 100% awake, you make better choices. No pressure to pick the right outfit. No panic to get dressed and run out the door. You wake up to a neat and tidy room. You don't come home to a disaster zone at night either, clothes strewn on the floor because you could not decide what to wear.

You are also more relaxed and save time.

Check tomorrow's weather. Ensure your selections do not hold you back, given the forecast. If the forecast calls for a warm day, make sure your choices won't leave you overheated. If it calls for rain or snow, ensure your outer layers protect your work clothes, and your footwear is appropriate. Pack a separate bag for your work shoes, if necessary.

Use a full-length mirror to make sure your choices work together.

Be complete. Select every single piece of clothing you want to wear the next day. This includes underwear, socks, belt and tie, as well as accessories like jewelry and a watch.

Be methodical and organized.

Put all your clothing choices on a hanger and hang it on a hook on the back of your closet or bedroom door. Use a large Ziplock bag to hold the smaller items, such as your jewelry and watch, and place it on the hanger as well.

Your wardrobe is now organized and in one place when you wake up tomorrow.

Iron your clothing the night before, if necessary, so all you need to do in the morning is put them on.

Plan Your Day's Tasks The Night Before

Spend five or ten minutes at the end of each day to plan tomorrow's work.

Write a list of the six most important tasks you must finish. If you can't come up with six, don't worry. Most days your list will probably contain only three or four items.

Organize your list so your most important job is at the top, followed by the second, and so on.

Write down how long you think it will take to complete each item on your list. These become your mini-deadlines throughout the day.

When you wake up in the morning, go over your list again. Refresh the importance of each item in your mind. Re-evaluate your time estimates. Make changes, if required.

When you begin your day, work on the first item on your list. Concentrate on it and complete it before you start the next one.

If you take all day to finish that one thing, no problem. It is more valuable to complete your most important job than to partially-complete many less important ones.

When you complete a task item, move on to your next one with the same focus and determination.

At the end of your work day, move any uncompleted tasks to tomorrow's list and create a new list of six tasks, sorted by order of importance.

Do this every day.

It is important to sort out your priorities the night before.

1. It prepares you for work, mentally and emotionally. Your unconscious mind goes to work on the problems right away and continues to resolve them while you sleep.

2. It's simple. You do it because it's easy. It becomes a success habit.

3. All your tough decisions are made while you are calm and relaxed.

4. It removes procrastination. When you don't know what to do next or you don't know what your most important task is for the day, you tend to procrastinate. When you begin your day with a clear list of priorities there is no confusion, no decisions to make. Just look at your list and start working.

5. It imposes a deadline for completion. Deadlines are powerful motivators and the closer the deadline, the more powerful its motivation. If your list contains six items and you must complete each task in 90 minutes or less, on average, to complete the list in an 8-hour work day.

6. It forces you to single-task. Multi-tasking is a myth perpetuated by unproductive people to rationalize their lack of accomplishments. When you focus your energy on a single task until it is complete, you finish it before you on to your next most important one.

> Successful, effective people are those who launch directly into their major tasks and then discipline themselves to work steadily and single-mindedly until those tasks are complete. "Failure to execute" is one of the biggest problems in organizations today.

> Many people confuse activity with accomplishment. They talk continually, hold endless meetings, and make wonderful plans, but in the final analysis, no one does the job and gets the results required. [11]

7. It forces you to do your most important task first, every day. Brian Tracy calls this eating your frog.

From his website:

> Mark Twain once said that if the first thing you do each morning is to eat a live frog, you can go through the day with the satisfaction of knowing that that is probably the worse things that is going to happen to you all day long. Your "frog" is your biggest, most important task, the one you are most likely to procrastinate on if you don't do something about it.[12]

Pre-Set Your Coffee Machine

If you drink coffee, set up your coffee machine the night before. If you use a Keurig machine, place your coffee pod beside it.

If you prefer a more traditional coffee maker, set the filter and coffee grounds the night before and set the machine's timer five minutes prior to your scheduled wake-up time. Use the sweet aroma of fresh coffee to draw you from the warm comfort of your bed.

If your coffee machine has no timer, preset the filter and grounds the night before. Then, when you haul your butt out of bed your only task is to press the Start button. Even the groggiest non-morning person (like me) can press a button.

Get a Solid 8 Hours of Sleep

I care less about my wake-up time than about the number of hours slept.
– Rachel Binx

Sleep deprivation impacts our concentration, our efficiency and our ability to make sound decisions.

It reduces our reaction time and the speed with which we make those decisions. It impairs our memory functions. It damages our immune system and leaves us susceptible to illness and disease.

Make a good night's sleep a priority in your life. In the hours before you go to bed, relax.

Do something enjoyable to help you wind down, so going to sleep is the last step in the natural progression of your day.

Avoid caffeinated drinks of any kind for at least 5 hours before you go to bed. Studies show it takes between 5 and 7 hours for half of the caffeine you ingest to leave your system and 8-10 hours for 75% of it to clear our bodies. Those numbers shocked me.

The Color Temperature of Light and Why It Matters

If you tend to be on your computer after dinner, I urge you to install the free program f.lux (https://justgetflux.com/).

Research shows all light hitting the eyes slows down production of Melatonin, the light-sensitive hormone that promotes sleep. It's our natural body clock that alerts our biological processes to the approximate hour of the day.[13]

Blue light waves (the primary wavelengths of sunlight) is particularly effective at reducing our body's natural production of Melatonin. This is where f.lux comes in. This great little program automatically adjusts the color temperature of light emitted from your computer screen to remove blue frequencies (daylight) and move them toward warmer tones more conducive to Melatonin production.

Become a Morning Person

When someone tells me to become a morning person a host of thoughts run through my mind.

Where did I leave the shovel?

Is there a backhoe nearby?

Where's the best place to dig a grave?

How deep should I make the hole?

My deep-seated disdain for mornings notwithstanding, peer-reviewed research slapped me across the face and confronted me with evidence to prove me wrong. Worse, my attitude worked against my desired output.

Research[14] published by the Journal of Applied Social Psychology confirms morning people are more proactive and productive than night-owls, like me.

> Proactivity is the willingness and ability to take action to change a situation to one's advantage and has been studied in a wide range

of contexts. The role of chronotype on proactivity has not been assessed. Individual differences in circadian rhythms have been widely acknowledged and are accepted as an interesting facet of human personality. Morning people were more proactive than evening types, and people with small differences in rise time between weekdays and free days were also more proactive persons. Sleep length (on weekdays and on free days) and total time spent in weekend oversleep did not show any relationship with proactivity. These results suggest that morning people are more proactive than are evening types.

Even I must grudgingly admit the truth. When I wake up early (yes, 8am is early) and get to work, I am more productive. I write more words. I write them easier and I write them faster than I do later in the day. I hate to admit it, given my contempt for mornings, but it's tough to argue against peer-reviewed research and my own personal experience.

Regardless, I still love how another author described his work day.

I keep writers hours. That means I wake up around noon and work through the night.

Wake up Naturally with Light

If possible, allow natural light to wake you up. Sunlight is our body's signal it's time to get out of bed.

This is not practical for most people. In the summer you would wake up at 4am, but in the winter you wouldn't get up until 8am or later. This is not conducive to keeping a job or maintaining a schedule.

As an alternative, buy an electrical timer switch and plug in your bedside lamp. When its time to wake up, the switch turns the lamp on - your signal to get out of bed. Bright indoor light tells your body clock the sun is up and it's time to get busy. Use daylight-balanced lights. They best mimic the blue spectrum of natural light, the trigger to shut down your body's Melatonin production.

If you absolutely must use your smartphone as your alarm clock, enable Airplane Mode before you go to sleep. This ensures you are not disturbed by email, social media notifications or inebriated pocket-dialers.

One option for your smartphone is the Sleep Cycle alarm clock app. From their website:[15]

How does it work?

Waking up easy is all about timing. Sleep Cycle alarm clock tracks your sleep patterns and wakes you up during light sleep. Waking up during light sleep feels like waking up naturally rested without an alarm clock.

Sleep Cycles

While you sleep, you go through cycles of sleep states. The first state in a sleep cycle is light sleep, followed by deep sleep and a dream state referred to as REM-sleep. A full sleep cycle lasts about 90 minutes and is normally repeated several times each night.

Your movements vary with each sleep phase. Sleep Cycle uses sound analysis to identify sleep states by tracking movements in bed. Sleep Cycle uses a wake up phase (30 minutes by default) that ends at your desired alarm time. During this phase Sleep Cycle will monitor signals from your body to wake you softly, when you are in the lightest possible sleep state.[16]

I started using Sleep Cycle two months ago and it confirmed what I've suspected for a long time - I don't sleep well. It helped me understand my sleep patterns and use that information to find ways to sleep more soundly.

Yes, I know. I just told you to keep your phone out of the bedroom. In my defense, I turn on Airplane Mode before I go to sleep so web notifications or phone calls can't bother me. If you decide Sleep Cycle is worth a try, I suggest you do the same.

Another interesting option is a wake-up light alarm clock. These clocks use light, not sound, to rouse you from slumber. They simulate the sunrise and gradually increase the intensity the light in your bedroom.

Some models even offer "natural sounds" - defined by one manufacturer as "piano, violin, bagpipe, waves, birds and 'DiDi'". What the latter means, neither Google nor I could discover and, unless you're Scottish, it's unlikely you consider the sound of bagpipes "natural!"

When you wake up to light and avoid the annoying sound of your alarm, you wake up a little calmer, a little more relaxed.

No Snooze Button

If you really think about it, hitting the snooze button in the morning doesn't even make sense. It's like saying, 'I hate getting up in the morning so I do it over… and over… and over again.'

– Demetrius Martin

The snooze button is the serial killer of your personal productivity. It is your mortal enemy. Most humans wield this weapon with stunning precision every morning, and to their detriment, because the quality of post-snooze button sleep is dubious, at best.

EosSleep researcher Dr. Matthew Mingrone[17] says, "Hitting the snooze button is, in fact, bad for sleep and can leave you groggier and more tired than initially getting out of bed after the first alarm. Instead of achieving an additional nine minutes of restful, deep sleep, our bodies endure nine minutes of light sleep."

Build a new habit. Get out of bed as soon as your alarm goes off.

This simple act delivers your first "win" of the day, and wields tremendous power over your life.

The night before, you made the decision to wake up at a certain time. You followed your decision with action - you hopped out of bed, as you promised you would last night. This simple formula - make a decision and follow it with action - is the key to success in every aspect of your life.

If you want to make your dreams come true, the first thing you have to do is wake up.

– J.M. Power

Drink One 16oz Glass of Water

Drink one 16oz glass of water as soon as you wake up to rehydrate, jump-start your digestive tract and flush toxins from your system. Your entire body benefits from water, the body's natural lubricant.

More important, it assists proper brain function.

Did you know your brain tissue is 76% water? Neither did I until I researched why drinking a 16oz glass of water first thing in the morning is a good idea.

Last summer we visited our children and grandchildren on Vancouver Island, where they played with their 4-wheel-drive, off-road RZR dune buggies. Coby, our youngest grandchild, handed me a helmet.

"Grandpa, you have to wear a brain bucket."

I dutifully tried to comply. I did not want to break the house rules, but their largest helmet did not fit me, so I teased him about it.

"Coby, my brain is so massive it won't fit inside the brain bucket."

It's now a running joke between us.

Seriously, though, if all it takes to protect my massive brain is to drink a glass of water each morning, I'm in!

Ignore Your Phone

"I find that checking my phone [in the morning] tramples over my positive vibes, because we all know that checking messages is like rattling a wasp nest."

– Stephanie Lee

In 2016, CareerBuilder.com[18] and Kaspersky Lab[19] (the anti-virus vendor) conducted independent studies of cell phone usage at work. Both studies came to the same conclusion - your smart phone distracts you from doing your job, splits your focus and breaks your concentration. It makes you less productive. Your phone is a time waster and focus breaker. Keep it far away from you until your first major task is finished or, as Brian Tracy says, you've eaten your first frog.

Check out Jeremy Goldman's list of 6 Apps to Stop Your Smartphone Addiction at https://www.inc.com/jeremy-goldman/6-apps-to-stop-your-smartphone-addiction.html

Exercise in the Morning

Billionaire Richard Branson says working out significantly boosts his productivity. He credits his 5am daily workout habit as the foundation of his own morning routine.[20]

His belief is backed by science. When you work out, your brain releases a chemical called brain-derived neurotrophic factor (BDNF), which improves brain function.

According to MakeYourBodyWork.com[21] there are seven primary benefits to a morning workout.

1. It enhances your metabolism.

When you exercise in the morning you burn more calories later in the day, *after you stop*, compared to those who do not exercise at all. You benefit from exercise once, when you work out, and again after you stop. Bonus points.

2. It cultivates a mindset of consistency (habit).

When you eat this frog first, you never miss a workout because you're "too busy."

3. It improves your physical and mental energy levels.

It's impossible to walk and be depressed at the same time.[22]

Morning exercise helps you set a positive mindset, regardless of your mood when you begin your workout.

4. It builds self-discipline (your attitude of determination).

As with most habits, exercise in the morning gets easier with time.

5. You get better sleep.

This claim is backed by research, according to Dr. Scott Collier, assistant professor in the Department of Health, Leisure and Exercise Science in Appalachian's College of Health Sciences.[23]

In every case, those who exercised at 7 a.m. experienced roughly a 10 percent reduction in blood pressure, a reduction they carried through the rest of the day. Their blood pressure also dipped about 25 percent at night, they slept longer, with more beneficial sleep cycles than when they exercised at other times of day.

6. Helps you achieve your fitness goals.

When you wake up early to exercise and forgo an extra 30 minutes of sleep, you are more determined to reap the reward for your sacrifice. This increases your personal determination to achieve your other goals as well.

7. Improves your love life.

Trainer Dave Smith says, "Do I even need to argue this one? You have created a strong habit of morning exercise, your metabolism is flowing, your body is looking and feeling better, you're sleeping well at night, and your mind is as sharp as ever."

He makes a valid point.

Eat a Healthy, Protein-Rich, Distraction-Free Breakfast

Without a healthy breakfast you force your body to run on empty. An engine cannot start without gasoline, so why would you force your body to run on fumes?

Breakfast provides your body and brain with fuel after an overnight fast. Focus on your food. Take the time to enjoy it. Make this your time of relaxation and rejuvenation.

What constitutes a healthy breakfast? The answer varies, depending on your definition of "expert" and their recommendations. I am not a health dietician, nor do I play one on television, so I won't deliver food advice here. Instead, I'll refer you to WebMD author Kathleen Zelman.[24]

Studies show a healthy breakfast helps give you:

1. A more nutritionally-complete diet, higher in nutrients, vitamins and minerals.

2. Improved concentration and performance in the classroom or the boardroom.

3. More strength and endurance to engage in physical activity.

4. Lower cholesterol levels

Research what constitutes a healthy breakfast for you and eat it every morning. Your brain will thank you. Your heart, too.

Take Only the Important Items Needed for the Day

If you carry a bag or backpack to work, take only those items you require today.

Contrary to popular myth, a backpack with every conceivable item is counter-productive. You waste a ton of time trying to find the one item you actually want. Pack only those items you need today. That way you can find what you need, when you need it.

Morning Checklist of Required Tasks

If you prepared your list last night, as I suggested earlier, now is the time to double-check it, both to add items you forgot and to re-evaluate your time estimates for each task. Your prioritized daily task list is critical to your productivity and long-term success.

Do you want to finish and publish your book within the next 12 months? Then review your action plan every morning until your book is on the bookstore shelf. Your glorious day of pride comes faster than you believe possible when you cultivate this simple habit.

Review Your Personal Vision Statement

Your vision statement is your unique productivity blueprint. It declares your purpose and builds self-discipline. It sets your course in life.

Review your personal vision statement every morning.

We all slip off the track sometimes, but when you do, use your vision statement to guide you back to the calm and protected waters of the Bay of Success. Use it to guide you through the stormy seas of opposition, procrastination and failure. Use it to guide you to the end of Publication Highway and your ultimate destination - your published book.

If you don't have a vision statement yet, I walk you through the entire process in great detail in the third book in the Author Success Foundations series - *Author Focus: How to Develop Your Personal Vision Statement and Advance Your Writing Career Beyond Your Wildest Dreams.*

http://ChristopherDiArmani.net/author-focus

Develop An Attitude of Gratitude

An attitude of gratitude is a fantastic way to start your day. Gratitude focuses your mind on your past successes. Feelings of gratitude shift you away from selfishness and self-centeredness, into a more positive and powerful mental state.

Wallace Wattles, in The Science of Getting Rich[25], states:

> The grateful mind is constantly fixed upon the best. Therefore it tends to become the best. It takes the form or character of the best, and will receive the best.

> Also, faith is born of gratitude. The grateful mind continually expects good things, and expectation becomes faith. The reaction of gratitude upon one's own mind produces faith, and every outgoing wave of grateful thanksgiving increases faith. The person who has no feeling of gratitude cannot long retain a living faith, and without a living faith you cannot get rich by the creative method, as we shall see in the following chapters.

> It is necessary, then, to cultivate the habit of being grateful for every good thing that comes to you and to give thanks continuously. And because all things have contributed to your advancement, you should include all things in your gratitude.

Tony Robbins, entrepreneur, best-selling author, philanthropist and the nation's #1 life and business strategist, gives his simple advice on this topic.

> Write down three things you are grateful for and meditate upon them for three and a half minutes.[26]

Not three. Not four. Three and a half.

> "I do three and a half minutes of pure gratitude about three things," Robbins says. "I pick one of those three to be simple... the wind on my face, my children's faces, anything."

> The reason he starts with gratitude, Robbins explains, is because of its ability to overpower the dangerous emotions that can sidetrack us.

> "The two emotions that mess us up the most are fear and anger, and you can't be grateful and fearful simultaneously. They

don't go together," Robbins says. "And you can't be angry and grateful simultaneously."

After spending a few minutes on gratitude, Robbins then shifts his focus to envisioning three larger successes he'd like to see six to 12 months down the line.

"I do three minutes of my 'Three to Thrive' - what are three outcomes or results I'm really committed to?" he poses.

"I see them as done and fulfilled ... When I feel it's fulfilled and done, I give thanks for it."

With three and a half minutes of focused gratitude under his belt, Robbins says he is primed for a positive day.

Sound advice from a man who transforms lives around the globe.

Write Someone a Thank-You Note

A thank-you note is an extension of the previous topic, gratitude. Your thank-you note is your expression of gratitude to someone for something they said, did or contributed to your life.

A thank-you note benefits your own mental health and forces you to think kind thoughts about someone other than yourself.

It also sets you apart in the mind of the card's recipient.

Nancy Olson, in her Forbes.com article *Five Reasons To Write Thank-You Notes*[27], explains.

1. It's the right thing to do.

2. It sets you apart.

3. Gratitude is good for the brain.

4. Handwritten letters perpetuate a very important part of our culture.

5. Jimmy Fallon does it.

While the last one may not be valid, the first four reasons work for me.

Meditation

Meditation is a positive act, and a daily positive mental health act is a powerful habit to cultivate.

Therapist Paul Thompson writes:[28]

> Meditation is a short cut on the path to experiencing God-consciousness. When one contacts God, all other objects of one's desire appear of themselves. "Seek first the kingdom of God... and all these things will be given you besides."(Matthew 6:33) There are a myriad of research studies on meditation that show benefits to health, sleep, mood and psychological growth. Here are some of the things that meditation can help us discover happiness, anxiety reduction, thought control, healing in our body and even material comfort.

Meditation helps clear your mind of clutter. Meditate for five minutes each morning to increase your productivity and mental acuity. The increased self-awareness and spiritual connection gained through meditation leaves you calmer, less stressed out and you sleep better at night.

Meditation forces you to be present, here and now, grounded in the moment. It opens your mind to the possibilities available to you. It inspires and rejuvenates you so when you start to work, you do so with more focus. This leads to a more productive day, and what author doesn't want that?

At the core of my morning routine is a self-hypnosis meditation designed to increase personal creativity.

I stumbled across Steven Luzern's free Hypnosis for Creative Writing[29] mp3 recording and listen to this every morning. If you seek more creativity, you may want to incorporate this mp3 into your morning routine, too.

Pray

Daily prayer sessions increase your attitude of gratitude. If you are a Christian or believer in some other faith, spend time in morning prayer to deepen your connection with God.

One of the biggest benefits of daily prayer is strengthened emotional and physical health.

According to a study, conducted by Dr. Crystal Park at the Department of Psychology at the University of Connecticut, those who pray regularly realize significant health benefits.

> Although both religion and spirituality were associated with better health behaviors at baseline in bivariate analyses, a proportional hazard model showed that only spirituality was significantly associated with reduced mortality risk (by 20%), controlling for demographics, health status, and health behaviors.[30]

This is impressive, as is the results of a study published in the Journal of Reward Deficiency Syndrome regarding prayer and substance abusers.[31]

> The strongest association between remission and spirituality involves attending religious services weekly, the one marker of the five that involves the highest social interaction/social bonding consistent with Durkheim's social bond theory.

> Conclusions: Stronger spiritual/religious beliefs and practices are directly associated with remission from abused drugs except crack. Much like the value of having a sponsor, for clients who abuse drugs, regular spiritual practice, particularly weekly attendance at the religious services of their choice is associated with significantly higher remission. These results demonstrate the clinically significant role of spirituality and the social bonds it creates in drug treatment programs.

This is not to say the only people who benefit from prayer are drug addicts and heart attack patients, nor do I imply all writers are drunks and drug addicts. Far from it!

Anyone who engages in regular prayer reaps these benefits. For writers, the calmer and more centered we are, the more productive, creative and powerful we become.

> Studies have suggested, however, that doing this [praying] with consistency helps improve calmness of the mind and body. And according to scientists, when this state of calmness is achieved, the body can apparently cope with sickness better, while the mind can deliver the feeling of a general sense of wellness.[32]

Despite all the research and study, nobody can adequately explain *why* prayer helps. We only know it does.

Read the Bible

When you read the Bible every day you derive many benefits, including peace of mind and deeper knowledge of God.

1. God's Word leads us to salvation.

2. The Scriptures guide our steps.

3. God's Word directs us to wisdom.

4. God's Word lifts our daily burden.

5. The Scriptures give peace.

6. It gives you the power to overcome sin.

7. It gives you direction and clarity for your future.

8. It brings you freedom from hurts, habits, and hang-ups.

9. It nourishes your soul.

10. It helps you grow your relationship with God.

11. You will know God better.

12. You will know yourself better.

13. You will discover answers to your biggest questions in life.

14. You'll discover some questions don't need to be answered.

15. It helps you grow in your relationships with other people, Christian and non-Christian alike.

This list could go on for days.

A humble and meek life is a reflection of God on earth, "And whoever exalts himself will be humbled, and he who humbles himself will be exalted."

– Matthew 23:12 (*The Bible – The New King James Version*)

Read Uplifting / Motivational Content

If you are not religious, you can derive many of prayer's benefits by reading uplifting and motivational content.

Read motivational quotes or passages from great historical figures to help cement your positive mindset for the day ahead.

"Humans are aspirational. We want to look up to role models and leaders and follow what they ask. Leaders and their words – inspirational quotes – affect us on a primal level," says Scott Sobel[33], founder of Media & Communications Strategies, Inc. in Washington, D.C.

When someone we respect and admire tells us our dream is possible, we want to believe them. We are more likely to implement and execute the strategies required to achieve success.

Tonight, before you go to bed, find a few motivational quotes or select a book to read for 15 minutes tomorrow morning. Do this every day and watch your attitude change for the better.

Ignore Email and Social Media

The distraction and intellectual noise of email and social media must be ignored in the morning.

Our subconscious mind picks up everything. It's a sponge. It drinks in every thought we encounter, without discernment or discretion.

Social media and its inherent nonsense promotes the worst aspects of our humanity at a time we should be focused on our creativity and peace of mind.

When email and/or social media is your mind's first input each day, you pour molasses on your brain synapses.

When you begin your day with Facebook and Twitter, you feed your ego and self-centeredness - two fatal blows to your mental health and productivity.

Nurture your attitude of gratitude, instead.

Ignore Television News

Television news fills your brain with negativity. Leave this time-sucking vortex turned off so it can't destroy your positive mindset.

The same is true when you come home after work. Leave the television turned off. Better yet, disconnect your cable service and toss out your TV. I do not recommend you give it to someone else. This would mean you condone the destruction of their lives with this insipid device and you don't want *their* failure on your conscience.

Ignore The Radio

If you must listen to something in the morning, try instrumental piano music or Gregorian Chant, music designed to sooth you and relax your mind. It helps you focus on the day ahead.

The garbage from radio, television or social media cannot write your book. Filling your mind with the failures and tragedies of tomorrow will not write your book either.

Read through your day's priority list. Focus on what you must accomplish today and assess the time you scheduled to complete each item. Revise it, if necessary.

Focus on the here and now, the most important tasks ahead of you today and the steps required to achieve your goal - a published book.

Spend Quality Time With Your Loved Ones

It's important to remember why we do what we do. We work hard to achieve success and provide the best we can for our family. Yes, our personal ambition plays a large part in our goals, but ultimately, every success we enjoy, every financial goal we achieve, is for our family.

If you have a spouse and children, spend quality time with them in the morning. Quality time with your family, even 15 minutes, gives you a positive experience you can fall back on throughout your day.

Never leave the house angry with your spouse or your children. You don't want a black cloud hanging over you all day, sucking every ounce of creativity and productivity from your mind.

Store your Purse, Wallet and Keys in the Same Place

How many times have you wondered where you left your keys, wallet or purse? For me, the answer is "way too many." I eventually learned what you already know. Leave my keys in the same physical location every time I come home.

If it means installing a key rack by the front door, do it. If a pretty bowl on an end table in the foyer is what floats your boat, fantastic. Which physical location you choose is irrelevant. The important point is to use the same physical location every time you come home. Be consistent.

This principle also applies to your wallet, purse, backpack or briefcase. Leave these items in the same place, so you know where to find them without thinking, every day.

Build a habit, a routine to eliminate these pointless searches from your life. The benefit? One less problem to solve before you leave home, and more time to build a productive foundation for the day ahead.

Store Your Weather Gear in the Same Place

Put your rain coat, umbrella and rain footwear in a single location. This eliminates another time-wasting search when the storm clouds roll in.

Your Daily Commute

You commute, so you need to be in your vehicle. That doesn't mean you should sacrifice this time on the altar of wasted years.

Turn your daily commute into education sessions. If you drive, load your vehicle with non-fiction audiobooks or podcasts. If you drive 30 minutes each way, you have an hour per day to learn new skills.

If you use public transit, even better. With no need to cope with traffic, you can focus on the new skill you want to learn or technique you want to try.

Load your iPod or MP3 player with audiobooks or some author-focused podcasts. Invest in a good set of noise-canceling earbuds.

For me, the MP3 player is the best invention ever. It's turned so much of my former non-productive time into awesome learning experiences.

The same is true for my daily workout. I use my MP3 player to get a double-benefit from it.

I love to compress time this way. This is also the only place where I advocate multi-tasking. One half hour on the stair-master or treadmill is mind-numbing. When I immerse my mind in a new skill or idea, I make productive use of the time my body performs repetitive tasks.

Two-for-one use of time is rare, so I grab the opportunity when I can.

Tell Yourself Positive Affirmations

An affirmation is a statement you say to yourself. Ideally, it is a positive statement designed to overcome our never-ending stream of negative self-talk. Positive affirmations tear out those weeds of self-doubt and recrimination and, in their place, sow healthy thoughts and ideas for your future.

Watch Jessica's Daily Affirmation on YouTube for an excellent example of a young girl repeating positive affirmations into the mirror (youtube.com/watch?v=qR3rK0kZFkg). She is adorable, and is an excellent example of how to set your own positive attitude for the day.

A positive affirmation, repeated in front of a mirror while you look into your own eyes, transforms your view of any personal, work, or self-love issue in a few days.

Consistent repetition over a lifetime will, as Steve Jobs explained to Standford University graduates in his 2005 Commencement Address[34], completely transform your world.

> When I was 17, I read a quote that went something like: "If you live each day as if it was your last, someday you'll most certainly be right." It made an impression on me, and since then, for the past 33 years, I have looked in the mirror every morning and asked myself: "If today were the last day of my life, would I want to do what I am about to do today?" And whenever the answer has been "No" for too many days in a row, I know I need to change something.
>
> Remembering that I'll be dead soon is the most important tool I've ever encountered to help me make the big choices in life. Because almost everything — all external expectations, all pride, all fear

of embarrassment or failure — these things just fall away in the face of death, leaving only what is truly important. Remembering that you are going to die is the best way I know to avoid the trap of thinking you have something to lose. You are already naked. There is no reason not to follow your heart.

If you don't know where to begin, here is a short list of affirmations you can use until you build your own.

1. The only limitations I have are the ones I place upon myself.

2. I control my feelings, emotions and responses to the events of my day.

3. I welcome today with love, gratitude and inner peace.

4. I am powerful and effective.

5. Today is the best day of my life.

6. Today is the most productive day of my life.

7. Facing today's challenges makes me stronger, more powerful and teaches me the lessons I need to learn to be my most productive self.

Record an Affirmation MP3 and Play It Every Morning

Why not record your positive affirmations with your smart phone? Then, when you need to reinforce your self-esteem and willpower, plug in your earbuds and play back the recording.

This is so much better than reading affirmations in silence. The voice you hear is your own, so you deliver an awesome message with the power of your own voice, whenever you need.

Record your answers to these questions:

- ❑ What do you believe in?
- ❑ What are your goals?
- ❑ Why do you want to achieve them?
- ❑ By what date do you want to achieve them?
- ❑ How do they make your life better?
- ❑ How does achieving these goals help someone else?

Listen to it throughout the day to keep yourself focused on the Big Prize.

Listen to Ambient Music at Work & When Writing

Would you believe listening to classical music, ambient piano sounds or Gregorian Chant will increase your daily word count? Me either - until I tried it for a week.

The results shocked me. I wrote more words in less time. I was also less mentally exhausted at the end of my writing sessions.

I'm a writer. I sit at my desk in silence and pound on my keyboard. It's what writers do. It's normal. I spent decades writing in silence, so it took time to break my silence habit. I still forget.

I find instrumental piano, Gregorian Chant (incredible stuff - try it!) or my latest obsession, Howler Monkeys roaring in a Costa Rican rainstorm, especially effective.

Oddly enough, my Howler Monkeys in the Rain audio track falls right in line with a *Business Insider* article[35] that says adding a natural sound element can boost your mood and your level of focus.

My anecdotal evidence is backed up by serious research, I discovered, and offers far more benefits than an increased daily word count.

Research published in France's Learning and Individual Differences[36], found students who listened to a one-hour lecture where classical music was played in the background scored significantly higher in a quiz on the lecture when compared to a similar group of students who heard the lecture with no music.

Reader's Digest[37] reported classical music offered a host of benefits to the listener, including lower blood pressure, better sleep, boosted brain power and better memory. Their article cites a number of studies to back up their claims.

A 2007 Standford University School of Medicine study[38] found music moves the brain to pay attention and helps it sort incoming information.

> The Stanford University School of Medicine research team showed that music engages the areas of the brain involved with paying attention, making predictions and updating the event in memory. Peak brain activity occurred during a short period of silence between musical movements - when seemingly nothing was happening.

In this foundational study, the researchers conclude that dynamic changes seen in the fMRI scans reflect the brain's evolving responses to different phases of a symphony. An event change - the movement transition signaled by the termination of one movement, a brief pause, followed by the initiation of a new movement - activates the first network, called the ventral fronto-temporal network.

Then a second network, the dorsal fronto-parietal network, turns the spotlight of attention to the change and, upon the next event beginning, updates working memory.

"The study suggests one possible adaptive evolutionary purpose of music," said Jonathan Berger, PhD, associate professor of music and a musician who is another co-author of the study. Music engages the brain over a period of time, he said, and the process of listening to music could be a way that the brain sharpens its ability to anticipate events and sustain attention.

Amisha Padnani, writing in the *New York Times*[39], echoed the results of these studies.

In biological terms, melodious sounds help encourage the release of dopamine in the reward area of the brain, as would eating a delicacy, looking at something appealing or smelling a pleasant aroma, said Dr. Amit Sood, a physician of integrative medicine with the Mayo Clinic.

Dr. Lesiuk's research focuses on how music affects workplace performance. In one study involving information technology specialists, she found that those who listened to music completed their tasks more quickly and came up with better ideas than those who didn't, because the music improved their mood.

"When you're stressed, you might make a decision more hastily; you have a very narrow focus of attention," she said. "When you're in a positive mood, you're able to take in more options."

While Costa Rican Howler Monkeys in the Rain may not be your thing, when I listen to these amazing critters roar it sends me straight to my happy place.

If this audio track interests you, drop me a request and I'll send you the MP3 file.

You may find it's the perfect alternative when you need a break from classical music or your own go-to audio backdrop.

https://ChristopherDiArmani.net/howler-monkeys-mp3

Devote 30 Minutes to a Hobby or Developing a Skill

Adopt the habit of spending 30-60 minutes each day to learn a new skill. This single change improved my writing overnight. It also flipped the switch on the whispering monster in my head who tells me repeatedly, *You're not a professional writer.*

Professional writers invest in themselves.

They devote blocks of time, every day, to educate themselves about the craft of writing. They devour books written by the masters of writing. How else can you steal what worked for the greatest authors in history and apply it to your own writing?

You can't.

Invest in yourself, your writing and your career.

Eat The Frog

"If it's your job to eat a frog, it's best to do it first thing in the morning. And if it's your job to eat two frogs, it's best to eat the biggest one first."

This quote is typically attributed to Mark Twain. The lack of evidence to back up this attribution does not, in any way, detract from the importance of the message.

So, what is this frog you must eat?

It's your most meaningful task. This is the one thing you most dread. It is the thing which, when completed, advances your career the furthest. It's also the thing you're most likely to procrastinate on. Whatever it is for you, do it first.

Once you eat the frog, your worst activity is over. Your day can only get better from here.

For me, the Frog of my morning routine is exercise, so I eat it first.

Exercise isn't the issue. No, the problem is the same as it is for writing.

Writing isn't difficult. Writing is easy.

I stumble over the simple part - beginning. I must plant my butt in the chair and turn on my computer.

I must start.

Exercise isn't the problem - starting to exercise - that's the beast I must slay each day.

If exercise is your morning demon, too, slay it as early as possible. Your heart will appreciate your sacrifice and your sense of satisfaction will power you through any trouble you face in the rest of your day.

Chapter 4

Build Your New Morning Routine

First Things First

Now the fun begins.

It's time to design your new morning routine.

Your score in the Morning Routine Test, combined with the list of actions you perform after you wake up each day, gives you all the information you need to build your new routine.

Grab your notebook and pen and sit down at your desk. Any table will do, so long as you give yourself a flat surface to write on.

If you prefer a pre-printed worksheet, download the PDF here:

https://ChristopherDiArmani.net/free-morning-routine-workbook

1. Write down every task you do now, from the time you wake up until you leave for work.

2. If you did not do so in Chapter 2, take the Morning Routine Test now. Write down your score.

3. Examine your current morning routine. Cross off at least one item from your list you know is detrimental to your positive mindset.

4. Examine the list of 28 Morning Habits of Highly Successful People. Select two actions to incorporate into your new morning routine.

5. Beside each item on your list, write down your estimate of how long it takes you to complete it.

For example, list brushing your teeth and taking a shower separately, and assign a time estimate to both. Repeat this process for every item on your list.

A healthy dose of patience serves you well throughout this process.

New habits take time to build. Start small and build on your successes. This ensures you remain in a calm and positive mindset - an essential component of any good morning routine.

You want to remove any possibility for a sense of failure to infiltrate your mind.

Your routine is not etched in stone. You can, and should, make changes as you are able. Don't push yourself. Remember, it takes two months for most people to build a new habit so it becomes automatic.

Review Your Scheduled Times Daily

Every day, note how long you take to complete each part of your new morning routine. Record those times beside each item. At the end of each week, compare your estimated times with your actual times. Make any adjustments required.

The key, at this point, is flexibility. Since it takes 66 days, on average, to build a new habit, perform the same task every day for at least two months before you evaluating whether the habit works for you or not. If it helps you be more productive, is it automatic and routine, or do you need more practice until it becomes second-nature?

New York wasn't built in a day. New and beneficial habits aren't built overnight either. Be kind to yourself as you build this new routine into a habit.

I found it difficult to stay focused, initially. Then, about a month into my new routine I discovered I got angry when it was interrupted. I took this as a great sign. It meant the new routine was important to me - important enough to get angry when I was interrupted.

It also meant I took this new way of life seriously. This pleased me greatly.

Adjust Your Routine as Needed

If one addition to your routine doesn't work for you, replace it with another action you think will work better.

Remember. It's your life. Mold this system so it works for you. The point is to improve your mindset and focus so you accomplish more every day.

Fill any empty blocks of time with a task from the list of 28 Morning Habits of Highly Successful People.

See how it goes for two months, until it becomes a habit.

Adjust again, as needed.

In two months time, evaluate how you feel at the start of your workday compared with how you felt before you started this program. Write and tell me about it. I want to hear your story.

https://ChristopherDiArmani.net/contact/

Chapter 5

Next Steps

What Now, You Ask?

With your new morning routine in place, it's time to figure out what you want from your writing career.

What we think about and where we devote our time - these are the things we value.

Do you write every day? The uncomfortable answer is probably "no," despite your best intentions. You've heard this advice before. Write every day. You've heard it so often the bile rises in the back of your throat. It's cliché. It's boring. It embodies everything we despise about writing advice, yet it is undeniably true. Ask any writer who earns a living with their words. They say the same thing.

Write every day.

Such simple advice. So hard to do.

Our problem is one of focus. We do not Follow One Course Until Successful.

It sounds so simple, doesn't it?

It is simple, but simple, as I stress repeatedly, does not equal easy.

Nothing good in life comes easy unless, perhaps, you win the lottery, but a big bucket of cash comes with a whole host of new problems.

If you want to write a book, but have not yet done so, well, we both know the problem, don't we?

No writer on earth "finds" the time to write. We must ruthlessly carve out chunks of time from our day, every day, without exception.

You must decide if writing your book is truly important.

Developing your Personal Author Vision Statement is an essential component of this decision.

The process demands you answer hard questions about who you are and what you want from your life. It demands you assess your personality, your values, and envision what your ideal life looks like.

The next book in the Author Success Foundations series, Author Focus: Develop Your Author Vision Statement and Laser-Focus Your Writing Career - along with your honest introspection - reveals, with absolute clarity, who you are and what you want from life.

Join me in the next step of your journey down Publication Highway.

Your ideal future awaits...

Purchase your copy of Author Focus here:

http://ChristopherDiArmani.net/author-focus

Purchase your copy of the Author Focus workbook here:

http://ChristopherDiArmani.net/author-focus-workbook

Download the Free Workbook

The Plan for Success is Written on Paper

Research by Dr. Gail Matthews at the Dominican University of California confirmed the results of a never-performed, but oft-cited Harvard or Yale study on the power of written goals. The mythical study claimed only 3% of the graduating class wrote down their goals and 20 years later out-earned their classmates by over ten times.

While not quite so earth-shattering as multiplied earning power, Dr. Matthews' study confirms when you write down your goals you are more liable to follow through and achieve them.

When you take one simple action and write down your goals, you increase your likelihood to follow through on your commitment and take the actions necessary to achieve your goals.

Pretty simple, right? Obvious, even, yet so many people do not write down their goals. They *decrease* their chances for success out of sheer laziness. That's crazy.

Download your free PDF copy of the Morning Routine Workbook.

Complete every exercise in this book to begin your day with a full gas tank of energy, enthusiasm and self-discipline to empower your writing life.

https://ChristopherDiArmani.net/free-morning-routine-workbook

The Road to Success Continues With Your Author Vision Statement

Do you struggle to "find time to write?"

No writer on earth "finds" the time. Time is not a commodity you earn but a finite resource you spend. Once spent, time cannot be recovered, recycled or reused. It's gone.

The issue is not our "lack" of time. The issue is our lack of focus.

Follow One Course Until Successful.

It sounds so simple, doesn't it?

It is simple, but simple, as I stress repeatedly, does not mean easy.

If your current path delivered the results you want, this book would not catch your eye. If doing what you've always done yielded success, you'd be writing your book right now instead of spending your precious time here, with me, in search of answers.

Read the third book in the Author Success Foundations series, *Author Focus – Develop Your Author Vision Statement and Laser-Focus Your Writing Career* to learn how creating your personal author vision statement will unlock the keys to your ideal future.

Available from your favorite online book retailers today.

For more information, visit:

https://ChristopherDiArmani.net/author-focus

One Last Thing!

First, thank you for reading this book!

If you enjoyed this book and found it informative (and even if you did not) I would be grateful if you would post an honest review on Amazon and/or Goodreads. Every review helps this book find more readers, the lifeblood of any author.

http://ChristopherDiArmani.net/review-morning-routine-amazon

http://ChristopherDiArmani.net/review-morning-routine-goodreads

Your support in the form of an honest review really does make a difference. Reviews help authors sell more books and I read every one as part of my efforts to make my books even better.

I would also be grateful if you shared a link to this book on your social media accounts.

If, for some reason, you did not like this book or didn't get what you expected out of it please tell me directly. I will use your constructive criticism to fix any flaws in my book so it better meets your expectations. Please contact me here:

https://ChristopherDiArmani.net/Contact

Thank you so much for your support, feedback and your honest reviews.

Sincerely,

Christopher di Armani

Author Extraordinare

About Christopher di Armani

"Author Extraordinaire"

Christopher di Armani is an Amazon bestselling author and the creator of Author Success Foundations.

This 7-book series teaches authors at any level how to develop the mindset, daily routines and work habits necessary to unleash their creativity and get their books published.

He has published 16 books and produced 4 documentary films on topics ranging from the craft of writing to civil liberties and politics.

Download your free introduction to the Author Success Foundations series at

https://ChristopherDiArmani.net/AuthorSuccessFoundations

Books by Christopher

Awaken Your Author Mindset: Finish Writing Your Book Fast (Author Success Foundations 1)

https://ChristopherDiArmani.net/author-mindset

https://ChristopherDiArmani.net/author-mindset-workbook

Learn how to develop your bullet-proof Author Mindset and create a system guaranteed to deliver success and to build the habits required to work this system every single day.

The choice is yours. If you continue to do what you've always done you'll just get what you already have, an unfinished manuscript and all the disappointment, discarded dreams and self-loathing you can handle.

You will never finish your book.

Now, imagine the possible...

Allow me to be your guide to help you construct a mindset, a solid foundation to complete your manuscript so published becomes, not just possible, but inevitable. This is the power of the Author Mindset.

Design Your Morning Routine: Jump-Start Your Writing Success (Author Success Foundations Book 2)

https://ChristopherDiArmani.net/morning-routine

https://ChristopherDiArmani.net/morning-routine-workbook

There is no magic to writing a book. None. You take action, every single day, until your book is finished. You plan, schedule and execute the plan. You write.

If you are serious about finishing your manuscript, grab your notebook, a pen, and a cup of your favorite beverage, and join me at the kitchen table. We'll chat about habits, willpower and self-discipline. We'll discuss how the mind functions, what makes a habit stick, and how our willpower fades throughout the day. We'll talk about concrete steps to improve your self-discipline.

Then I'll ask you to complete a series of exercises. These exercises reveal, at a deep level, what's important to you - what you value most in life. This clarity of purpose allows you to create a morning routine designed to jump-start your daily writing output.

Author Focus: Develop Your Author Vision Statement and Laser-Focus Your Writing Career (Author Success Foundations Book 3)

https://ChristopherDiArmani.net/author-focus

https://ChristopherDiArmani.net/author-focus-workbook

Writing is easy. Finishing your book is easy, too.

Focus. Be diligent. Apply self-discipline and determination.

You already possess these qualities. This book would not appeal to you if you didn't.

Your author vision statement is an extraordinary targeting mechanism to guide you to your ultimate destination - the end of Publication Highway.

The exercises ahead serve one purpose - to focus your mind on what you value most - your published book.

Join me and map your personal journey down Publication Highway. Discover what you value most, not just in writing, but in your entire life.

Isn't your ideal future worth the time?

Prolific Author: The Step-by-Step Guide to Write More Words in Less Time and Finish Your Book Fast (Author Success Foundations 4)

https://ChristopherDiArmani.net/prolific-author

https://ChristopherDiArmani.net/prolific-author-workbook

The key to unlock your drive to succeed is knowing why you write. When you understand how your desire to write fulfills your core needs, you transform writing from a chore to be dreaded into the vision you were born to fulfill. Time set aside to write becomes as critical to your life as the food you eat and the water you drink.

If we believe success does not matter, neither does the road we travel to get there.

Success matters. The road you travel to achieve success matters more.

Your daily writing routine is the last piece of the puzzle to build a life focused on accomplishing your goal - a finished and published book.

Done is Better than Perfect: 7 Keys to Finish Writing Your Book Fast (Author Success Foundations 5)

https://ChristopherDiArmani.net/done-better-perfect

Give Up Your Perfectionism and Publish Your Book

The three fundamental truths of writing are:

1. Your book will never be perfect.

2. You cannot publish what you do not complete.

3. Done is better than perfect.

Learn how to finish your book easier, faster and better than you ever thought possible when you apply the Seven Keys of Writing Success.

Become Unstoppable: 7 Habits of Highly Successful Authors (Author Success Foundations Book 6)

https://ChristopherDiArmani.net/become-unstoppable

Success leaves clues.

Figure out what successful authors did to advance their careers, then do what they did. It's the most effective course of action. Simple concept, but we must do the work. You know, the hard part.

In the pages ahead I discuss how each habit works, as well as the lies we tell ourselves to rationalize our lack of forward progress. Finally, I shine the light of truth on the lies we tell ourselves and watch as they scurry away like little cockroaches.

Apply these principles to your life and you'll achieve their success. It's inevitable. All it takes is a pinch of perseverance, a dash of focus, and two cups of hard work.

I Don't Have Time To Write And Other Lies Writers Tell Themselves (Author Success Foundations Book 7)

https://ChristopherDiArmani.net/no-time-to-write

Stop Lying To Yourself.

In this installment of the Author Success Foundations series, I dissect seven lies writers tell ourselves and shine the light of truth upon each one.

Every falsehood obscures a truth we refuse to confront. The job of a writer, any writer, is to face our fears head on, protected by the body armor of honesty and integrity. Only then does the brilliance we etch on the page shine bright for the world to see.

Each delusion corrodes holes in our armor, holes the insidious demons of worry, self-doubt, procrastination and perfectionism slip through to poison us.

The Author Success Foundations series provides the tools and materials to patch those holes, to reinforce and strengthen our armor. The day of battle is here, and we must march ever forward. If we stop, even for a moment, our words shrink under the oppressive heat of our fears and we fail.

Step inside. Face your fears. Show these pathetic demons you cannot be cowed. Own your internal dialog and reshape it into a powerful engine, then use that power to drive down Publication Highway.

The Simple 3-Step Secret to Slaughter Writer's Block And Vanquish it Forever

https://ChristopherDiArmani.net/Writers-Block-Book

There is no more perfect Hell than one where I cannot write. You know that terror, too, don't you? That sense your last remaining creative spark abandoned you some time back. It's sickening.

Let me show you how to extricate yourself from that "perfect Hell" permanently.

TOP SECRET - Inspiration, Motivation and Encouragement - 701 Essential Quotes for Writers

https://ChristopherDiArmani.net/Top-Secret-Quotes

This compilation of 701 quotes delivers inspiration, motivation and encouragement on 39 aspects of writing and the writing life.

You will discover quotes to make you laugh and quotes to make you cry. Some are familiar, like old friends. Others you will meet for the first time. All have a common theme: The Writing Life.

When you need it most, you will find words of encouragement here.

Filming Police is Legal - How to Hold Police Accountable While Staying Out of Jail

I write about police issues regularly. I highlight good cops when I can, but I focus on the problems in our police forces with honesty, integrity and abuse. Every time news breaks about police seizing another citizen's camera or cell phone I receive the same question.

Christopher, is it legal to film police?

The unequivocal answer is a court-affirmed YES. It is legal to film police in every state in the United States of America and in every single province and territory of Canada. That YES comes with specific caveats for the audio portion of a recording depending upon your jurisdiction, and it is critical you know those caveats.

The purpose of this book is to educate mere citizens and police forces alike about the legality of the right of citizens to film police, along with an examination of the legal history supporting our legal right to do so.

https://ChristopherDiArmani.net/Filming-Police

Justin Trudeau - 47 Character-Revealing Quotes from Canada's 23rd Prime Minister and What They Mean for You

On October 19, 2015 Canadians elected their 23rd Prime Minister based on good looks, nice hair and a famous name.

They voted for style over substance.

Our 23rd Prime Minister's entire leadership experience consisted of teaching snowboarding lessons and high school drama. His management experience consisted of administering his trust fund and his ego.

Not a single thought was given to what he stood for, what his party stood for, or what he would actually do once elected to the highest office in the land. That bothered me. That bothered me so much I began to research his much-publicized missteps and that in turn revealed a disturbing pattern within Trudeau's numerous faux pas. That pattern is the focus of this book.

https://ChristopherDiArmani.net/Justin-Trudeau-Book-1

From Refugee to Cabinet Minister: Maryam Monsef's Meteoric Rise to Power and her Spectacular Fall From Grace

Maryam Monsef is the ultimate immigrant success story. She could not speak English when she arrived in Canada at age eleven. Two decades later she became Canada's first Muslim Cabinet Minister.

Maryam Monsef's story begins with her mother, a young Afghan widow who fled Afghanistan for Canada with her three young daughters in 1995. That widow spoke English but her three daughters did not. They brought something far more valuable to Canada: the unshakeable belief they could accomplish anything they wanted, so long as they worked hard.

It's no accident her belief in herself led Maryam Monsef to a Cabinet post. She worked hard to learn English and graduated from Trent University, an impossible accomplishment in her native Afghanistan.

Maryam Monsef became the unwitting scapegoat for Trudeau's broken promise on electoral reform, a promise he knew he would break by May 2016. Her birthplace controversy, her attempts to discredit and insult her electoral reform committee, combined with the Prime Minister's betrayal of her trust, sounded the death knell of her political career.

This, then, is the story of one young woman's meteoric rise to political power. It is also the story of that young woman's undoing at the hands of a narcissistic and self-serving celebrity feminist, Justin Trudeau.

https://ChristopherDiArmani.net/Maryam-Monsef-Book

Endnotes

1   Maltz, Dr. Maxwell. "Psycho-Cybernetics: Updated and Expanded." Tarcher-Perigee, Nov. 3 2015. Digital Edition.

2   Gardner, B., Lally, P., & Wardle, J. (2012). "Making Health Habitual: The Psychology of Habit Formation and General Practice." The British Journal of General Practice, 62(605), 664–666. http://doi.org/10.3399/bjgp12X659466

3   Lally, P., van Jaarsveld, C. H. M., Potts, H. W. W. and Wardle, J. (2010), "How Are Habits Formed: Modelling Habit Formation in the Real World." Eur. J. Soc. Psychol., 40: 998–1009. doi:10.1002/ejsp.674

4   Gardner, Ben. "Busting The 21 Days Habit Formation Myth." Research Department of Behavioural Science and Health Blog, June 29, 2012, http://blogs.ucl.ac.uk/bsh/2012/06/29/busting-the-21-days-habit-formation-myth/. Accessed: Jan. 10, 2018.

5   Baumeister, Roy F. "Willpower: Why Self-Control is the Secret to Success." Penguin Press, 2011. Digital Edition.

6   ibid.

7   Shai Danziger, Jonathan Levav, Liora Avnaim-Pesso. "Extraneous factors in judicial decisions." Proceedings of the National Academy of Sciences Apr 2011, 108 (17) 6889-6892; DOI: 10.1073/pnas.1018033108

8   The Economist. "I think it's time we broke for lunch...." The Economist, Apr. 14, 2011, http://www.economist.com/node/18557594. Accessed: Feb. 03, 2018.

9   Baumeister, Roy F. "Willpower: Why Self-Control is the Secret to Success." Penguin Press, 2011. Digital Edition.

10   Angela L. Duckworth and Martin E. P. Seligman, "Self-Discipline Outdoes IQ in Predicting Academic Performance of Adolescents," Psychological Science 16 (2005): 939–44.

11   Tracy, Brian. "Eat That Frog: Brian Tracy Explains the Truth About Frogs." BrianTracy.com, Undated, https://www.briantracy.com/blog/time-management/the-truth-about-frogs/. Accessed: Jan. 09, 2018.

12   ibid

13   Beil, LAURA. "In Eyes, a Clock Calibrated by Wavelengths of Light." The New York Times Company, July 4, 2011, http://www.nytimes.com/2011/07/05/health/05light.html?_r=2&pagewanted=all. Accessed: Jan. 09, 2018.

14   Randler, C. (2009), Proactive People Are Morning People1. Journal of Applied Social Psychology, 39: 2787–2797. doi:10.1111/j.1559-1816.2009.00549.x

15   https://www.sleepcycle.com/how-it-works/

16   https://www.sleepcycle.com/how-it-works/

17   Vanderkam, Laura. "That Snooze Button Habit Is Putting Your Productivity To Sleep, So Quit Hitting It." Fast Company, Oct. 7, 2013, https://www.fastcompany.com/3019389/that-snooze-button-habit-is-putting-your-productivity-to-sleep-so-quit-hitting-it. Accessed: Jan. 09, 2018.

18   CareerBuilder. "New CareerBuilder Survey Reveals How Much Smartphones Are Sapping Productivity at Work." CareerBuilder, Jun 09, 2016, https://www.prnewswire.com/news-releases/new-careerbuilder-survey-reveals-how-much-smartphones-are-sapping-productivity-at-work-300281718.html. Accessed: Jan. 06, 2018.

19   Kaspersky Lab. "Kaspersky Lab Study Proves Smartphones Distract Workers and Decrease Productivity." Kaspersky Lab, August 26, 2016, https://usa.kaspersky.com/about/press-releases/2016_kaspersky-lab-study-proves-smartphones-distract-workers-and-decrease-productivity. Accessed: Jan. 06, 2018.

20   Ward, Marguerite. "Richard Branson says this daily habit doubles his productivity." CNBC.com, Nov. 10, 2016, https://www.cnbc.com/2016/11/10/richard-branson-says-this-daily-habit-doubles-his-productivity.html. Accessed: Jan. 06, 2018.

21   Smith, Dave. "7 Benefits of Morning Exercise, Plus 5 Tricks To Actually Love It." MakeYourBodyWork.com, Undated, https://makeyourbodywork.com/benefits-of-morning-exercise/. Accessed: Jan. 09, 2018.

22   Fox, Kenneth R.. "The influence of physical activity on mental well-being." Journal of Public Health Nutrition, Volume 2, Issue 3a, March 1999 , pp. 411-418, https://doi.org/10.1017/S1368980099000567. Accessed: Jan. 09, 2018.

23   ASU News. "Early morning exercise is best for reducing blood pressure and improving sleep." Appalacian State University News, June 13, 2011, http://www.news.appstate.edu/2011/06/13/early-morning-exercise/. Accessed: Jan. 09, 2018.

24   Zelman, MPH, RD, LD, Kathleen M.. "The Many Benefits of Breakfast." WebMD.com, Undated, https://www.webmd.com/diet/features/many-benefits-breakfast#1. Accessed: Jan. 09, 2018.

25   Wattles, Wallace. "The Science of Getting Rich." WikiSource.org, 1910, https://en.wikisource.org/wiki/The_Science_of_Getting_Rich. Accessed: Jan. 09, 2018.

26   Capretto, Lisa. "The Morning Ritual That Helps Tony Robbins Stay Positive All Day." OWN, Sep 05, 2016, https://www.huffingtonpost.com/entry/tony-rob-bins-morning-ritual_us_57c4ae57e4b09cd22d922f78. Accessed: Jan. 09, 2018.

27   Olson, Nancy. "Five Reasons To Write Thank-You Notes." Forbes.com, Jan 22, 2017, https://www.forbes.com/sites/nancyolson/2017/01/22/five-reasons-to-write-thank-you-notes/#635cd5172811. Accessed: Jan. 09, 2018.

28   Thompson, Paul. "Meditation: Silent Prayer." PaulThompsonTherapy.com, Undated, http://paulthompsontherapy.com/the-practice-of-meditation/. Accessed: Jan. 10, 2018.

29   Luzern, Steven. "Hypnosis For Creative Writing." Steven Luzern international, Undated, http://stevenluzern.org/product/hypnosis-creative-writing/. Accessed: Jan. 12, 2018.

30   Park, C. L., Aldwin, C. M., Choun, S., George, L., Suresh, D. P., & Bliss, D. (2016). Spiritual peace predicts 5-year mortality in congestive heart failure patients. Health Psychology, 35(3), 203-210. http://dx.doi.org/10.1037/hea0000271

31   Schoenthaler, Stephen J. et al. "NIDA-Drug Addiction Treatment Outcome Study (DATOS) Relapse as a Function of Spirituality/Religiosity." Journal of reward deficiency syndrome 1.1 (2015): 36–45. PMC. Web. 10 Jan. 2018.

32   Unilab. "The Power of Prayer and Meditation – Unilab." unilab.com.ph, July 16, 2015, about:reader?url=https%3A%2F%2Fwww.unilab.com.ph%2Farticles%2Ft-he-power-of-prayer-and-meditation%2F. Accessed: Jan. 10, 2018.

33   Moran, Gwen. "The Science Behind Why Inspirational Quotes Motivate Us." Fast Company, Sep. 25, 2015, https://www.fastcompany.com/3051432/why-inspira-tional-quotes-motivate-us. Accessed: Jan. 10, 2018.

34   Jobs, Steve. "Commencement address delivered by Steve Jobs." Stanford University, June 14, 2005, https://news.stanford.edu/2005/06/14/jobs-061505/. Accessed: Jan. 10, 2018.

35   Gillett, Rachel. "The best music to listen to for optimal productivity, according to science." Business Insider Inc., Jul. 24, 2015, http://www.businessinsider.com/the-best-music-for-productivity-2015-7. Accessed: Jan. 10, 2018.

36   Engel, Allison. "Studying for finals? Let classical music help." USC News, Dec. 5, 2014, https://news.usc.edu/71969/studying-for-finals-let-classical-music-help/. Accessed: Jan. 10, 2018.

37   Nelson, Brooke. "10 Wondrous Things That Happen to Your Body When You Listen to Classical Music." Reader's Digest, Undated, https://www.rd.com/health/wellness/classical-music-effects/. Accessed: Jan. 10, 2018.

38   Baker, Mitzi. "Music moves brain to pay attention, Stanford study finds." Stanford Medicine, Aug. 1, 2007, https://med.stanford.edu/news/all-news/2007/07/music-moves-brain-to-pay-attention-stanford-study-finds.html. Accessed: Jan. 10, 2018.

39   Padnani, Amisha. "The Power of Music, Tapped in a Cubicle." The New York Times Company, AUG. 11, 2012, http://www.nytimes.com/2012/08/12/jobs/how-music-can-improve-worker-productivity-workstation.html. Accessed: Jan. 10, 2018.

Made in the USA
Las Vegas, NV
06 November 2024